My Journey to You

BY
KIZZY K GARRICK

My Journey to You

Copyright © 2024 by Kizzy Garrick

All rights reserved. No part of this book may be reproduced, distributed, or transmitted in any form or by any means, including photocopying, recording, or other electronic or mechanical methods, without the prior written permission of the publisher, except in the case of brief quotations embodied in critical reviews and certain other noncommercial uses permitted by copyright law. For permission requests, write to the publisher, addressed "Attention: Permissions Coordinator," in the email below.

xpressivekween@gmail.com

Cover design by Kizzy Garrick

Printed in the United States of America

First Edition, 2024

Scripture quotations are taken from the Holy Bible, New International Version® NIV®. Copyright © 1973, 1978, 1984, 2011 by Biblica, Inc.™ Used by permission. All rights reserved worldwide.

Dedication

To my amazing husband, Leon: This book is dedicated to you. Your unwavering support, love, and strength have been the bedrock of our journey. You stood by me through every challenge, lifting me when I felt defeated and celebrating every small victory. Your belief in us and our dream of becoming parents never wavered, and I am eternally grateful. Thank you for being my rock, partner, and best friend.

To my miracle baby, Kingston Isaiah Noel Garrick (KING): You are the inspiration behind this book. Watching you grow over the past four and a half years has been the greatest joy of my life. Your laugh is infectious, and your smile can brighten up any room. You have such a kind, gentle soul;

your vocabulary and curiosity amaze me daily. I can't wait to see your future, my sweet boy. Your presence in our lives is a constant reminder of the miracles that faith and perseverance can bring. You are loved and cherished, and your role in our lives is invaluable.

To my mother: Thank you for always telling me to trust God. Your faith and wisdom have been a guiding light, helping me stay strong and believe in the power of prayer. Your constant encouragement and love have been invaluable. I am deeply grateful for your presence in my life and the wisdom you have shared. Your role in my journey is significant and deeply appreciated.

To my sister: Thank you for always having hope. Your positivity and support have kept me motivated and optimistic. Your belief in me and our dream has strengthened and inspired me.

To my best friend: Your unwavering hope and encouragement have shone light during my darkest days. Your constant support, laughter, and love have carried me through moments of doubt and fear. Thank you for being my confidant, cheerleader, and sister in spirit. Your friendship is a cherished gift, and I am forever grateful.

With all my love, I dedicate this book to you all.

Table of Contents

Preface — 9

Introduction — 12

Chapter 1: Beginnings — 17

Chapter 2: First Signs of Trouble — 23

Chapter 3: Medical Mysteries — 26

Chapter 4: Further Complications — 31

Chapter 5: Seeking Help — 39

Chapter 6: The Long Wait — 45

Chapter 7: The Miracle Happens — 51

Chapter 8: Motherhood Begins — 57

Chapter 9: Trusting in God — 63

Chapter 10: Conclusion 68

Final Thoughts and Encouragement 72

Preface

About eight years ago, I had the idea to write a book about relationships, detailing the perils of dating and the joy of finding your spouse. However, the words wouldn't flow. Looking back, I understand that God had different plans for me. Fast forward to December 2018: while in the shower, I received what seemed like a message—*My Journey to You,* my unborn child. It was the title of my book, but I wasn't pregnant. How could I write a book about my unborn child when I wasn't even expecting it?

Two months later, I was pregnant, and getting there was a journey. The more I shared my story with others, the more I realized I was not alone. Many people face similar challenges, and the solidarity and support I found were invaluable.

This book is my way of sharing my journey to become a mother. It was a path marked by medical challenges, emotional hurdles, and unwavering faith. From being told I would never have children to dealing with prolactinoma, PCOS, and ulcerative colitis, each step was a testament to the power of hope and determination. Writing this book has required me to be the most vulnerable I've ever been, opening up about my deepest fears, struggles, and triumphs.

Through prayer, the support of my loving husband, and the encouragement of friends and family, I overcame the obstacles that stood in the way of my dream. *My Journey to You* is not just a story about my path to motherhood but a testament to the strength within each of us when faced with seemingly insurmountable odds.

As you read this book, I hope it gives you the courage to face your challenges, the reassurance that you are not alone, and the inspiration to keep believing in miracles. My Journey to You is my story, but it is also a story for anyone who has ever faced adversity and found the strength to overcome it.

Thank you for joining me on this journey.

With love and gratitude,

Kizzy

Introduction

Motherhood is a journey filled with hope, challenges, and moments of profound joy. My journey to becoming a mother was no different, marked by unexpected obstacles and the unwavering support of loved ones. I always dreamed of having children when I got married. Growing up in a single-parent household, I wanted a different experience for my unborn children. Coming from a big family, I aimed to have at least four kids— two boys and two girls. The typical dream, right? But as I grew older, that number started to dwindle. I went from wanting four to three to two, eventually settling on even one shot with twins.

I married in 2014 at 34, and my husband and I eagerly decided to start a family. However, what began as a hopeful and exciting time soon became a series of medical challenges that tested our patience and resilience. In August of that year, I missed my menstrual cycle and, filled with anticipation, took a pregnancy test. To my disappointment, it was negative. A visit to my primary care doctor confirmed that I was not pregnant, but this began a series of medical discoveries shaping my path to motherhood.

Despite the endless medical challenges I faced, my faith in God, the unwavering support of my husband, and the encouragement from my family and my best friend kept me going. With the help of my specialist, I started on a journey of medical treatments, lifestyle changes, and weight loss to improve my chances of conception. Each step was a testament to my faith and the power of hope and perseverance.

Finally, after years of struggle and heartache, I received the joyous news of a positive pregnancy test. The journey that once seemed so distant culminated in the birth of my beautiful baby boy. This book is a testament to that journey—a story of faith, determination, and the incredible support system that helped me achieve my dream of motherhood.

This book aims to share my journey of motherhood with others who are facing similar challenges. During my baby shower, I was approached by several people who thanked me for sharing my story because they were silently dealing with the same issues. By sharing my story, I hope to offer support, encouragement, and a sense of solidarity to those who are struggling to conceive or are dealing with complex medical issues. I also want to inform others that just because a woman is of a certain age, they should stop asking when she will have a baby. It may not be a question of when, but if she can, or even if she wants one. My journey is a reminder that, despite the obstacles and setbacks, it is possible to achieve your dreams with faith, perseverance, and the support of loved ones.

To those reading this book, I want you to know that you are not alone. The road to motherhood can be long and hard but is filled with moments of hope and joy. Trust your journey, lean on your support system, and believe that brighter days are ahead. Remember that every step brings you closer to your dream, no matter how difficult the path may seem. Keep believing, keep hoping, and never give up. When "man" says no, remember that God has the final say. Your miracle is just around the corner.

Chapter 1: Beginnings

After a whirlwind courtship, I married my husband in April 2014. Our wedding was not a big fancy affair; it was just the two of us, along with my sister, my niece, and my baby great-niece. We married at the courthouse, and I wore an A-line halter white cocktail dress. I felt nervous as we left the parking garage for the courthouse. It wasn't the act of getting married that made me uneasy; it was walking through the parking lot in a white dress while heading to the courthouse. I felt like I was on display and couldn't help but wonder what people might think. Would they say, "Oh, she's getting married at the courthouse"? It's funny how we let such invasive thoughts cloud moments that should be purely joyful. It's the same with the persistent question, "When are you going to start having kids?"—sometimes, you want to enjoy the present moment.

As it turned out, the dress I was nervous about became a hit. Another couple was in full wedding attire, accompanied by their wedding party and guests. Seeing them made me realize that it doesn't matter what people think on your special day. I received compliments on my dress from other couples and even the judge. I remember the judge saying, "This is the prettiest dress I've seen," she also commented that we were the cutest couple. Despite the small setting, we married in a cozy room with other couples waiting outside for their turn.

Instead of a big wedding, my mother threw us a fantastic wedding party at her home. Everyone was there to celebrate our union. I remember someone saying during the party, "It's time to start making babies." I was excited for the next chapter of our lives, though I had yet to learn it would be long and challenging.

After settling into married life, my husband and I decided to grow our family. My husband already had a son, my beloved bonus son, and we talked about adding two more children to our family. We both hoped our first child would be a girl joining her big brother. We spent many evenings discussing baby names, nursery themes, and how we envisioned our lives with our future children. It was a time filled with hope and dreams, and we felt ready to take on the new adventure of parenthood together.

We also discussed the practical aspects of starting a family. We considered our financial stability, our home environment, and how we would balance our careers with raising children. We knew it wouldn't be easy, but we were determined to create a loving and supportive home for our future children. We felt confident in our ability to overcome any obstacles that might come our way.

The initial excitement and anticipation of starting a family filled our days with hope and dreams for the future. We couldn't wait to share the news with our family and friends. We spent hours imagining how we would tell them—should I show up pregnant one day? The thought of their joyful reactions and the love surrounding our growing family made us giddy with anticipation. Every month brought a new wave of excitement as we hoped for a positive pregnancy test.

During the first months of our marriage, we attended two baby showers. I could see my new husband's excitement, only imagining what our shower would be like. In my free time, I often browse baby shower ideas and potential nursery designs. I couldn't walk past a baby aisle without oohing at the adorable little outfits.

Our anticipation grew with each passing day, and we found ourselves daydreaming about holding our baby for the first time, hearing their first laugh, and watching them take their first steps. The vision of our future family brought us immense joy and motivated us to keep moving forward despite any challenges we might face.

However, as we soon learn, the road to parenthood is often unpredictable and filled with twists and turns. While our initial excitement was unwavering, we soon faced challenges that tested our patience, resilience, and faith. But through it all, we held onto our dream of becoming parents, knowing that the journey would be worth it, no matter how difficult.

Chapter 2: First Signs of Trouble

In August of 2014, a few months after our wedding, I missed my menstrual cycle. Filled with eagerness and hope, I took a pregnancy test. I'll admit, I kept a few tests in the bathroom cabinet for moments like this. After checking the results, I was disappointed to see it was negative. I decided to try again first thing in the morning, as I had read somewhere that your first sample tends to be more accurate. However, I later learned that Human Chorionic Gonadotropin (HCG), the pregnancy hormone, can be detected as early as 10-12 days after conception, so it really wouldn't have mattered what time of day I took the test.

The next morning, I took another test, but it was still negative. I chalked it up to having stored the tests in the cabinet too long. I was extremely late, having wholly missed my menstrual cycle, so I couldn't understand how I wasn't pregnant. Determined to discover what was happening, I made a doctor's appointment with my primary care physician (PCP).

During the visit, my PCP confirmed that my pregnancy test was negative. I was confused and frustrated—how could I not be pregnant after trying so hard and having no menstrual cycle? My PCP advised me to wait and see if I missed my cycle the following month. If I did, he suggested I give the office a call, and he would prescribe something to induce my cycle.

When I missed my cycle for the second month in a row, I called my PCP back. True to his word, he said he would send a prescription to my pharmacy to bring on my cycle. That suggestion did not sit well with me. I've never been one to take medication without an apparent reason, and I felt uneasy about inducing my cycle without understanding the underlying cause of my missed periods.

As I left the doctor's office that day, a sense of unease settled over me. I knew this was just the beginning of a journey that would be far more complicated than I had ever imagined. Little did I know that medical discoveries and challenges would fill the future, testing my patience, resilience, and faith.

Chapter 3: Medical Mysteries

Anxiety and uncertainty filled the weeks following my initial doctor's visit. When my menstrual cycle still didn't return, I knew something wasn't right. It was time to dig deeper and discover what was happening with my body. What started as a hopeful journey to motherhood quickly became a quest for answers and a struggle to understand my health.

I decided to make an appointment with a gynecologist (GYN) to understand better why I was missing my cycle. I anxiously awaited the results of numerous tests during my initial visit. A couple of days later, I received a call from the GYN office while I was at work. Naturally, I stepped outside my shared office space to take the call. I was numb and confused by what I was hearing. When I returned to my office visibly shaken, my manager, standing at the back of the room, noticed my distress. I made it to my desk and told my colleagues about the call.

The nurse referred me to an endocrinologist. To be transparent, I did not know what an endocrinologist specialized in then. I probed to find out why I needed to see one, but the nurse was vague. Sensing my unsettledness, she finally stated that I had an enlarged pituitary gland but couldn't provide further details, insisting I needed to see the endocrinologist.

My small group of colleagues, including my manager, were incredibly supportive, assuring me everything would be okay. However, I couldn't shake the feeling that something was wrong. I went from thinking about motherhood to worrying about my health. For those who may not know, the pituitary gland is a small gland located at the base of the brain. In my case, I showed signs of an enlarged gland.

At that moment, while everyone was trying to comfort me, I became an internet doctor. I searched for everything I could find on why I would need an endocrinologist and what could cause an enlarged gland. I came across the word "tumor" in my search, and all I could think of was a brain tumor. Being an internet doctor is not always the best course of action. I had to stop myself, collect my thoughts, and decide how to inform my husband.

My husband was very supportive and accompanied me to my first endocrinology appointment. My endocrinologist performed an exam, ran some tests, and scheduled me for an MRI. The day of my MRI appointment was when I learned I was possibly claustrophobic. Fear overtook me, and I was unable to complete the MRI. My endocrinologist had to prescribe me something to take the morning of my next MRI appointment and change the location to a facility with an "open" machine. Thank goodness for the prescription because the second machine was not open, but I slept like a baby.

The MRI results came back, and the results showed that I had a benign tumor in my brain. Simply put, my body produced high levels of prolactin, causing the enlargement of my pituitary gland. My body was making breast milk even though I was not pregnant. The medical term for this condition is prolactinoma. Some of the symptoms include milky discharge from the breasts, which I rarely had, but my breasts were always tender to touch, low sex drive, infertility, and irregular or missed cycles. The recommended treatment option from my endocrinologist was daily medication to help reduce the tumor, with a follow-up MRI within a year. To think, if I had allowed my PCP to prescribe me the cycle-inducing medication, I would not have discovered this when I did.

Chapter 4: Further Complications

With the diagnosis of prolactinoma came a new set of challenges. While I began my treatment and hoped for the best, I soon found out that my journey to motherhood would encounter even more obstacles. Unexpected turns laid ahead, and I had to navigate each patiently and resiliently.

By now, it had been a year since my diagnosis. After completing my second MRI, my endocrinologist stated that the tumor had shrunk to the point it was barely visible on the MRI. However, he wanted me to continue the medication and follow up in six months. I was hopeful that my journey to motherhood was back on track.

One of my colleagues recommended a new GYN, someone she had visited. She expressed that this GYN was more sympathetic to her patients' needs, and the office staff and environment were much more personable than my previous GYN. While at a checkup with my regular PCP, I remember sitting in his office, explaining why I had declined a pap smear exam because I was going to see the new GYN to discuss possibly having kids.

I was stunned by the words that followed next. In a very unsympathetic, matter-of-fact tone, the doctor said, "You will never have kids." As I write these words today, I feel the same way I did then. I was fighting to hold back my tears but was crying inside. All I could think at that moment and now is, how can a doctor, not just anyone, but a doctor, be so insensitive to his patient? Where are your manners? I was in a state of shock, and the words didn't come out. All I wanted to do was hurry and get out of that office.

Fast forward to my visit with the new GYN; she was charming and welcoming. I shared my medical history with her as well as what my PCP had said. She assured me not to worry and that it was still possible to have a baby. After the exam, she broke the news to me: I had Polycystic Ovary Syndrome, commonly known as PCOS. PCOS is a hormonal disorder that can lead to infertility. Some physical symptoms I had but did not know were attributed to PCOS at the time included strands of hair near my jaw, occasional dark skin patches by my neck, irregular periods, extreme pelvic pain, and weight gain. I initially attributed the weight gain to being newly married. Another symptom, which is unnoticeable, is insulin resistance. Because of this, my GYN prescribed me medication. However, the medication, which was a diabetic medication, was not to cure PCOS but to manage it since there is no cure.

A PCOS diagnosis, combined with prolactinoma, meant my chances of having a child were diminishing. However, she gave me a glimmer of hope, saying there was still a possibility of pregnancy, but I would need to see a fertility specialist.

Meeting with the fertility specialist, two things stood out more than the invasive fertility exam. One was that I was going through a form of depression. After a series of questions, she suggested I might be experiencing depression, although I didn't feel it. My lack of motivation, desire to watch television more than work out (something I used to do before the pregnancy journey), lack of interest in leaving the house some days, and poor eating habits were signs. Another symptom of PCOS is craving sweets and salty food, which are signs of insulin resistance, and I was craving them, resulting in my additional weight gain. The other point was that to start any fertility treatment, even to be prescribed a pill, I would need to lose weight. But how could I lose weight when my body was fighting against me? The glimmer of hope I had was starting to fade away.

If I mentioned this before, I'll repeat it: my husband was so supportive during this journey. I never questioned God but asked, "What can I do? How can I overcome some of these challenges?" The answer was right in my home: it was my husband. He said he would help me lose weight. In the evenings, we started walking in the park, and on weekends, we would climb Stone Mountain. Not knowing much about nutrition, I started eating what I thought was healthy: high fiber, protein, lots of green veggies, salads (which were my go-to meal), and little carbs. I even made smoothies for breakfast, which contained juice and fruits. Little did I know my healthy eating was not 100% healthy.

While on this "healthy journey," I often needed to go to the bathroom. Once, while shopping in the supermarket, I remember leaving my cart in the middle of the aisle and hurrying to my car, praying I would make it home in time. I became so fearful of eating out, not knowing if I would have the urge to go to the bathroom. When I did go, sometimes all I would see were clots of blood. "What is wrong now?" was the thought that crept into my mind.

I scheduled a visit with my PCP, who suspected it might be hemorrhoids, but couldn't find anything during the exam. He referred me to a gastroenterologist. Here we go, another specialist likely to bring more bad news—that's all I kept thinking. Unfortunately, I was right. After a colonoscopy, I was diagnosed with ulcerative colitis (UC), an inflammatory bowel disease affecting the intestines. When I asked, "How did I get this?" The answer was vague; it's unknown how one contracts UC, and although it's not curable, it is manageable with long-term medication. Some food triggers for UC include high-fiber foods such as fruits and vegetables, sugar, and spicy foods—there went my go-to salad meals, smoothies, and favorite spicy dishes.

Another important question I had was whether I could still get pregnant. My doctor informed me that it was possible to conceive with UC when in remission. However, if my UC was not in remission, meaning I was experiencing a flare-up, it would be difficult. Moreover, getting pregnant during a flare-up could increase the risk of miscarriage. Talk about feeling defeated.

Chapter 5: Seeking Help

By this time, it had been two years, and I had received three life-changing, non-curable diagnoses: prolactinoma, PCOS, and ulcerative colitis. Despite all these setbacks, I refused to give up. The next step in my journey was to seek specialized help and explore all possible options. With my husband by my side and a renewed determination, I knew that no matter how many obstacles stood in our way, we would find a way to overcome them and achieve our dream of becoming parents.

I needed to make a lifestyle change, starting with my health. The only thing I had control over was my weight. If I could control my weight and eat the right foods—avoiding the sweets and salty foods my PCOS made my body crave and steering clear of high-fiber foods and sugar that would trigger my UC—I could improve my chances. I focused on what the fertility specialist said: if I lost weight, I could start fertility treatment. My goal was to have a baby, so I needed to take the steps to get help. I was already taking medication for my prolactinoma, PCOS, and UC.

Years before marriage, when I initially moved to Georgia, I gained weight and reached my heaviest. I considered weight loss surgery back then and knew a few people who had undergone the procedure. I attended an hour-long presentation but decided it wasn't for me. Instead, I fell in love with the gym. I started working out and even hired a trainer. I got back in shape and felt great about myself. However, this time around, it became harder to lose weight. My healthy eating seemed to backfire, and my body craved foods detrimental to my health.

After speaking with my husband, I decided to give weight loss surgery another chance. This time, I listened intentionally during the presentation. The surgeon mentioned that some people get pregnant after surgery, even though the recommendation is to wait about 18 months—it happens. After the presentation, I scheduled a one-on-one session with the surgeon. What I loved most about the surgeon I chose was her ability to listen and provide me with options, but ultimately, the decision on the type of surgery was mine.

Now, I could have continued to work out with no avail, but my goal was to get healthy and lose weight to start fertility treatment. With all my medical issues, it seemed like the only way. Many people think weight loss surgery is the easy way out. It is a tool, and like any other tool, you have to use it appropriately for it to work. One of my requirements before weight loss surgery was attending nutrition classes once a month for six months. During that time, I learned about healthy eating and the importance of moderation. I discovered that too much of a good thing might not be good. I learned I could still have sweets, maybe once a week instead of every day. I understood the right sugar content for a healthy snack, such as a protein bar or a cup of yogurt. I still read labels in the grocery store, which takes me longer than average. The most important thing I learned is that I still must put in the work.

I had my surgery in February 2017. While recovering at home, I started walking—first to the end of the block, then to the next block, and eventually to the end of my subdivision. As soon as I got the clearance to go to the gym, I was there five days a week. When not at the gym, I was walking on my lunch break. I would even park my car at the end of the parking lot and walk to where I needed to go. I couldn't eat much because of the surgery, but what I did eat was 100% healthy, and I 100% avoided anything that would hinder my goal, which was having a baby.

Through sheer determination, unwavering support from my husband, and a disciplined approach to my health, I felt more prepared than ever to embark on the next phase of our journey to parenthood. The path was still challenging, but I was determined and committed to overcoming obstacles.

Chapter 6: The Long Wait

As I focused on my health and well-being, the wait for positive news felt endless. Each step forward brought new hope but also new challenges. The road to parenthood was far from straightforward, and the lessons learned along the way were invaluable. Despite the uncertainties, we held onto our dream, knowing that every effort brought us closer to achieving it.

By the fall of 2018, my health had significantly improved. My prolactinoma was under control with medication, and my third MRI showed that the tumor was no longer visible. However, my endocrinologist recommended that I continue the medication. Though I had minor symptoms of PCOS, I chose to stop taking the medication.

Managing my UC medication was a struggle for months, but my gastroenterologist finally found a medication that worked for me, and I was in remission.

One day, I had a conversation with my sister, and she shared that her friend had used a pregnancy app to aid in getting pregnant. Curious, I scoured the app store for one that would fit my needs. In November 2018, I found an app that tracked my menstrual cycle based on the data from the previous months. The app estimated my next cycle and included my highest ovulation dates and the least likely days to get pregnant. Based on the information I inputted, it worked for December and January; my cycle was on time.

Going into the New Year, I decided to fast. One of my reasons for fasting was to get closer to God. During my fast, I gave up social media and meat—two things consuming my time and body. I wanted to focus on starting the journey to having a baby. I wanted to be spiritually and mentally ready before making another appointment with the fertility doctor.

The journey to motherhood was filled with emotional ups and downs. There were moments of hope and joy, followed by periods of doubt and despair. Every doctor's visit was a blow, but I learned to cope with the disappointments through various strategies and support systems.

My faith in God was a cornerstone of my resilience. I prayed regularly and sought comfort in my spiritual beliefs, which helped me maintain hope. My husband was an unwavering source of support, always there to lift my spirits and encourage me to keep going. We leaned on each other during the tough times, and his belief in us motivated me.

I also found solace in talking to close friends and family members who understood our journey. Their encouragement and empathy provided a sense of solidarity and reminded me that I was not alone. To cope with the stress and emotional toll, I developed several strategies. I practiced mindfulness and meditation, which helped calm my mind and focus on the present moment. Exercise became a therapeutic outlet, providing a sense of control and release. Walking, yoga, and even simple stretching exercises helped me stay physically and mentally balanced. When planning my 40th birthday, my best friend and I would joke that we would either be in Greece celebrating my birthday or I'd be home celebrating a baby shower. Her unwavering support and humor lightened the burden and gave me hope.

Support groups were another vital resource. Connecting with others who were going through similar experiences provided a sense of community and understanding. Sharing stories, challenges, and triumphs created a comforting and empowering bond.

Maintaining hope and perseverance was crucial. I kept reminding myself of the ultimate goal and the joy that awaited us. Visualizing our future family and the happiness we would share kept me motivated. I also celebrated small victories like health improvements and positive lifestyle changes.

Despite the emotional rollercoaster, I remained determined. Each setback reminded me of my strength and resilience. I learned to appreciate the journey, knowing that every step brought us closer to our dream of becoming parents.

Chapter 7: The Miracle Happens

As the months went by, the combination of faith, determination, and the right tools started to pay off. Little did we know the miracle we had been praying for was just around the corner. The journey was far from over, but we were finally on the brink of achieving the dream that had kept us going through all the challenges.

By February 25th, I should have had my cycle according to the app. Out of curiosity, I grabbed a pregnancy test from the cabinet. There was a very faint, barely visible line indicating pregnancy. My husband was excited—he had predicted the day we conceived—but I was skeptical since we were a day outside my ovulation window. Still uncertain, I took a picture of the test and sent it to my best friend. She replied with joy, but I was still doubtful. She suggested I take another test. Wanting a clear answer, I decided to pick up a digital test after work.

Anxiousness filled the entire day at work. I may have shown one of my friends at work, who also confirmed the test was positive. Despite their assurance, I was still in disbelief. After work, I spent twenty minutes looking for the best test in the pregnancy aisle. I was too anxious to wait until the following day. I took the test and waited as soon as I got home. POSITIVE—the test said POSITIVE. I dropped to my knees and said, "Thank you, Father GOD," and then I began to jump for joy. I couldn't wait for my husband to return, so I called him to share the news. He was ecstatic and said, "I already knew." All our plans to creatively share the news with family and friends went out the window. I took a picture of the test and sent it to my mother, sister, and best friend.

Before sharing the news with more people, I wanted confirmation from the doctor. I scheduled a visit, and my PCP, the same one who said I could never have children, confirmed I was indeed pregnant. You might wonder why I still saw that PCP. Well, everything happens for a reason. He is no longer my PCP, but he served his purpose. Despite his lack of bedside manners, he was a good doctor, and for some unknown reason, I couldn't let him go until I had my pregnancy confirmation.

I had planned a trip with my best friend, not knowing I would be pregnant. It was our annual beginning-of-the-year trip. The day after my doctor's appointment, I boarded a plane to Atlantic City with my best friend. I was so sick—I lost my voice and was the most congested I had ever been. I decided not to plan any more trips because I did not want to be sick and away from home.

Due to my previous medical concerns, I had to visit all my specialists. When I told my gastroenterologist I was pregnant, he asked why I didn't consult with him first. I responded, "It wasn't me; it was God's timing." I must clarify that my gastroenterologist was concerned about my health and wanted to ensure I was in remission. He remains one of the best doctors I have ever had and truly cares about his patients.

Since surgery, my morning breakfast has consisted of healthy smoothies made with water or almond milk, greens like spinach or kale, fruits, and protein powder. When I informed my surgeon about my pregnancy, she advised switching to solid breakfasts and ensuring I was taking my vitamins.

In addition to my previous specialists, I had to see another specialist monthly because I was considered high-risk due to my medical history and age. Despite these precautions, my pregnancy was relatively easy. Besides being congested and losing my voice early on, I had no major issues other than swollen feet and some fatigue.

As we prepared for the arrival of our baby boy, the reality of our miracle began to set in. The road had been long and challenging, but every step brought us closer to the joy we now felt. Our journey was a testament to faith, perseverance, and the incredible support system surrounding us.

Chapter 8: Motherhood Begins

The due date for my unborn baby was November 1st. I was selfishly excited about that date because my birthday is in November, and my husband's and bonus son's birthdays are also in November. So, I was determined to have a November baby against doctors' orders. Let's rewind a bit.

My doctor told me I would never have children due to my health conditions and age. My doctor told me I would not carry to full term. The obstetrician specialist strongly recommended that I have my baby at 39 weeks. After a lot of back and forth with the doctors and praying every night, I decided to be induced at 39 weeks. My obstetrician scheduled my inducement for the evening of October 24th. That day, my mom cooked me a wonderful meal since I couldn't eat later. I arrived at the hospital ready to be induced. I checked in and waited for the nurse to take me to my room. By 6 pm, my nurse induced me with a vaginal insert to soften my cervix. At 3:06 pm on October 25th, this little miracle popped out, literally popped out, and landed on my stomach. The doctor might have placed him there, but it felt like he landed on my stomach. I finally met and held the little miracle baby I had dreamed about for five years.

The early days of motherhood were a mix of joy and challenges. I had dealt with prolactinoma, where my body prematurely produced breast milk. Now, as a mother, I had the most challenging time breastfeeding and an even harder time pumping. My baby didn't latch on while in the hospital. A lactation specialist tried to assist, but it didn't work. One of the on-call physicians suggested my baby might have a tongue-tied—a condition where the tongue is not lifting from the bottom of the mouth. This condition could explain why he wasn't latching on to the breast. She recommended speaking with his pediatrician after discharge, as surgery might be necessary.

The first night home with our new little one felt like the longest night of my life. The morning we left the hospital was hectic. The photographer was setting up for the photo shoot, the pediatrician came in for the final check, the lactation specialist wanted to follow up, and the nurse needed me to complete paperwork for the birth certificate. The little one started to get fussy, and my husband kicked everyone out of the room except the pediatrician.

We finally made it home around mid-afternoon, after a quick stop to pick up some formula since I was still having trouble breastfeeding. As we settled in for the evening, my husband finally decided to put the bassinet together. It's not like we had nine months. LOL. After assembling the bassinet, my husband thought the mattress might be too hard for the baby. Our little one must have felt that way because he did not want to sleep in the bassinet.

Our precious newborn cried ALL night. As soon as I placed my head on the pillow, the crying awakened me. When I glanced at the clock, only 10-15 minutes had passed. I wanted to call my mother for help, but it was

2 am, and I knew she was sleeping. I tried everything to calm him down, but he would not stop crying. My husband ended up lying on the bedroom floor with our baby on his chest. That's how we got through the night.

The following day, my mother advised me that the little guy was in a new environment—at home—and out of his comfort zone. I know that making the transition seamless is crucial for the next baby. Maybe try recreating some of the noises and lighting in the new room.

As I reflect on my journey to motherhood, gratitude and amazement fill my thoughts as I consider the challenges we overcame. From being told I would never have children to dealing with multiple health issues, each obstacle seemed impossible. But we made it with determination, faith, and the support of my incredible husband and family. Motherhood had officially begun, and despite the sleepless nights and early struggles, it was everything I had hoped for and more.

Becoming a parent was a long road filled with unexpected turns, but it taught me resilience, patience, and the importance of never losing hope. Each moment, each challenge, brought us closer to this beautiful reality. And as I held my baby boy, I knew every step of the journey had been worth it.

Chapter 9: Trusting in God

Throughout my journey to motherhood, my relationship with God was a constant source of strength and guidance. In the face of numerous medical challenges and emotional setbacks, my faith provided a foundation that helped me persevere.

I leaned on my faith after being told I might never have children. There were days when the news was too heavy, and it felt like the world was closing in on me. During those moments, I found solace in prayer and scripture. Jeremiah 29:11 became my anchor: "For I know the plans I have for you, declares the Lord, plans to prosper you and not to harm you, plans to give you hope and a future." This verse reassured me that despite the hardships, God had a plan for my life; it included hope and a future.

My husband is also a praying man, and he told me many nights he asked for strength, guidance, and the blessing of a child. Our shared faith brought us closer, reinforcing our bond and giving us the resilience to face each challenge head-on. I always trust God, mainly when medical setbacks occur; our faith keeps us grounded and hopeful.

There were several pivotal moments where faith and prayer played a crucial role. When I was first diagnosed with prolactinoma, the fear of the unknown was overwhelming. I remember praying an entire night, asking God for peace, and understanding. The next day, I felt an unexplainable calm wash over me. This peace allowed me to approach my treatment positively, believing that God was in control.

Another significant moment was during my weight loss journey. Losing weight was essential for starting fertility treatments, but it felt like an impossible task. I prayed for strength and discipline, and God answered by giving me the determination and support I needed. My husband and I began walking together, and each step felt like a prayer in motion, moving us closer to our goal.

When I finally saw the positive pregnancy test, it was a moment of pure joy and gratitude. I fell to my knees, thanking God for this miracle. Throughout my pregnancy, I continued to pray for the health and safety of my baby. I earnestly prayed for the best outcomes at each doctor's visit and ultrasound, seeking strength and blessings.

As I reflect on my journey, several inspirational quotes and scriptures stand out:

- "Faith is the assurance of things hoped for, the conviction of things not seen." - Hebrews 11:1. This verse reminded me to hold on to my faith, even when the outcome was uncertain.
- "Cast all your anxiety on Him because He cares for you." - 1 Peter 5:7. I would remember this verse and surrender my worries to God whenever I felt overwhelmed.
- "I can do all things through Christ who strengthens me." - Philippians 4:13. This scripture was my mantra during difficult times, reminding me that I

could overcome any obstacle with God's strength.

Looking back, I see how every challenge and setback was a part of God's plan to strengthen my faith and prepare me for motherhood. Trusting in God didn't mean the journey was easy, but it assured me that I was never alone. Each prayer and each moment of faith brought me closer to realizing my dream.

My journey to motherhood is a testament to the power of faith and the importance of trusting in God's plan. It reminds me that even in our darkest moments, there is a higher purpose at work. By leaning on my faith, I found the strength to persevere, the courage to face each challenge, and the joy of witnessing a miracle.

Chapter 10: Conclusion

As I reflect on the journey to motherhood, I am overwhelmed with gratitude and awe at the path that brought us to our miracle baby. What began as a hopeful, exciting time soon became a series of medical challenges that tested my patience, resilience, and faith.

It started with the heartbreaking news of a negative pregnancy test and a missed menstrual cycle in August 2014, followed by the shocking diagnoses of prolactinoma, PCOS, and ulcerative colitis. Each diagnosis felt like a significant setback, but with each challenge, I found new strength in my faith and the unwavering support of my husband and loved ones.

Navigating through prolactinoma, my faith in God became my anchor. Prayer and scripture provided solace and hope, while the support from my husband reinforced our bond and determination. Despite the medical hurdles, I refused to give up on our dream of becoming parents. Seeking specialized help, I underwent weight loss surgery, attended nutrition classes, and committed to a healthier lifestyle to improve my chances of conception.

The journey to motherhood included emotional ups and downs, yet I maintained hope and perseverance. By the fall of 2018, my health had significantly improved. My prolactinoma was under control, my PCOS symptoms had lessened, and my UC was in remission. A conversation with my sister led me to a pregnancy app that accurately tracked my cycle, and in February 2019, our prayers came through with a positive pregnancy test.

Though marked by initial skepticism and frequent visits to specialists, the pregnancy journey was a period of immense joy and anticipation. Our baby boy arrived on October 25th, a bit earlier than my desired November due date, but his arrival brought unparalleled happiness. The early days of motherhood were challenging, with difficulties in breastfeeding and adjusting to our newborn's needs. Still, the love and support from my family helped us navigate these initial hurdles.

Throughout this journey, my relationship with God provided constant strength and guidance. Moments of faith and prayer sustained me during the darkest times, and inspirational scriptures like Jeremiah 29:11 and Philippians 4:13 kept me hopeful and resilient. Trusting in God's plan, even when the road seemed challenging, allowed me to persevere and ultimately realize our dream of parenthood.

Final Thoughts and Encouragement for Readers

To anyone reading this book who may be facing similar challenges, I want you to know that you are not alone. The road to parenthood can be long and demanding, filled with unexpected twists and turns, but it is also a journey of immense growth and discovery. Trust your journey, lean on your support system, and believe that brighter days are ahead.

Never underestimate the power of hope and determination. Each setback is an opportunity to grow stronger, and every challenge brings you one step closer to your dream. Remember to celebrate small victories along the way and believe that miracles happen.

Your journey may be difficult, but it is also uniquely yours. Embrace it with faith, perseverance, and an open heart. Keep believing, keep hoping, and never give up. When "man" says no, remember that God has the final say. Your miracle is just around the corner.

Made in the USA
Columbia, SC
20 October 2024